Debt Free Forever

How to Clear Your Debts, Manage Your
Money, & Become Financially Free

Steven E. Dunlop

DEDICATION

This book is dedicated to my beautiful and loving
girlfriend, Danni.

CONTENTS

ACKNOWLEDGMENTS

The insights in this book have been passed down to me
from a number of inspirational people who I have had the
good fortune of meeting. This book could not have been
written without you and my life would not be on the path
it is now. I am eternally grateful to everybody who has
positively impacted my life and I wish to share your
wisdom here in these pages through my words. Thank you
to all, you know who you are..

DISCLAIMER

No part of this publication may be reproduced or transmitted in any form by any means, mechanical or electronic, including photocopying or recording, or by any information storage and retrieval system, or transmitted by email without permission in writing from the publisher. Reviewers may quote brief passages in reviews.

While all attempts have been made to verify the information provided in this publication, neither the author nor the publisher assumes any responsibility for errors, omissions, or contrary interpretations of the subject matter herein.

This book is for entertainment purposes only. The views expressed are those of the author alone, and should not be taken as expert instruction or commands. The reader is responsible for his or her own actions.

Adherence to all applicable laws and regulations, including international, federal, state, and local governing professional licensing, business practices, advertising, and all other aspects of doing business in the US, Canada, or any other jurisdiction is the sole responsibility of the purchaser or reader.

Neither the author nor the publisher assumes any responsibility or liability whatsoever on the behalf of the purchaser or reader of these materials.

Any perceived slight of any individual or organization is purely unintentional.

How to Clear Your Debts, Manage Your Money, & Become Financially Free

INTRODUCTION

I want to thank you and congratulate you for purchasing the book, "Budgeting Secrets when you're Broke".

This is a quick-to-read guidebook that contains proven steps and strategies in 5 mini chapters on how save money when you're broke and on a budget.

It might be difficult to save cash at any point; however, it's especially challenging when you feel as if you're broke. If you are barely able to afford your expenses and you're living from paycheck to paycheck, saving cash probably is amongst the last thing on your mind. But, it is still possible to save cash when you are broke. As a matter of fact, saving cash, even if it's a little, is an important measure to cease in being broke.

So long as you're making some income, you ought to be saving some. Particularly if you regularly have insufficient funds, it is vital that you make a habit of saving cash. In spite of the fact that you possess little additional funds, there are methods of saving. Cutting expenses, sticking with a budget, and saving up a little at a time all are methods you can use to save money, yet there are additional ways, too. The following chapter includes 5 ideas that you should consider.

Thanks again for purchasing this book, I hope you enjoy it!

CHAPTER 1

CUT OUT ANY EXTRAS

One simple method of saving money when you are broke includes cutting costs. You might think there isn't anything you have the ability to initially cut out, yet think a bit harder. If you're really "broke," you have to let a few things go. Do you actually have to have such a pricy smart phone plan? What about your cable TV? Are you able to use the Internet at your local library or utilize WiFi rather than paying a month-to-month charge? There are multiple things, which we consider necessities that really are mere extras, and slashing some of these is going to rapidly free up more funds. Take a peek at your month-to-month expenses, and determine what really is necessary. If you have a desire to cease in being broke, you might need to trim a few of the extras for a little while.

Also, you may have to assess your spending habits. Merely selecting a generic brand of food, or using coupons or shopping deals quickly can save you cash. You might need to slash your preference for name brand products to save big.

Action Steps:

Cut These Ten Unnecessary Purchases Consuming Your Budget.

1. Convenient drinks and snacks
2. Beauty products
3. New clothing
4. Overpriced hotels
5. Media, books, and movies
6. Apps
7. Latest technology
8. Cable television and landlines
9. Gym memberships
10. Auto loans

CHAPTER 2

MAKE DINNER AT HOME

Getting lunch on the run is a lot more convenient and easier than bringing your lunch to work, yet doing this on a regular basis really will eat away at your budget. Dining out is a typical way individuals get into personal debt, according to Living on a Dime. It is simple to rationalize dining out because you're too busy to prepare dinner, or you're a poor cook. But, preparing food at home truly will save you cash, and if you have a desire to save money, you have to make the effort and time needed to cook at home.

Action Steps: It's possible to save time by preparing multiple meals over the weekend and then freezing them to eat within the workweek. If you just do not know how to cook, purchase a cookbook for beginner cooks.

CHATER 3

MAKE OUT A BUDGET

If you do not have a budget, step one should be to create one. Maybe you already created a budget, yet there are many reasons a budget might fail. If you lost your job recently, or somehow your income changed yet you're utilizing the same budget, you'll have to create a new one. Also, you might have to look at the budget and check if it really is reasonable and if you should adjust something.

If you're broke and on a tight budget, there will include **several steps** which may help, according to Lifehacker.

Action Steps:
Begin by evaluating your financial situation, trim costs (as pointed out in Chapter One), be

frugal. There will include other measures to take, which includes paying down debt.

CHAPTER 4

SAVE MONEY A LITTLE AT A TIME

If you are completely broke, the concept of saving anything potentially feels unreasonable. But, you need to get into the habit of saving money if you're going to save more within the long term. It is important that you consider the future: jot down your financial objectives, even if these goals seem thoroughly out of reach. Next, begin to save. If you aren't saving anything right now, any savings will be an improvement. As you trim extras and begin to follow your budget, it is possible to use a bit of the discretionary cash to save for the future.

Action Steps:
An additional idea includes getting a second job. Even if you just work a couple of additional

hours every week, yet you place all of the money into a savings account, you quickly will witness a change in your financial circumstances.

CHAPTER 5

AVOID TYPICAL MISTAKES

It is possible to make plenty of great decisions concerning your finances; however, if you make a couple of poor decisions, you still will have a difficult time saving. A few of the worst things you can do as you're broke involve splurging anytime you get a little money, taking on too much debt, prioritizing convenience, or making bad decisions about debt, having no savings whatsoever, or living beyond your means.
It really is simple to live beyond your means, yet it's one of the simplest methods of getting into debt. If you possess a difficult time controlling spending, attempt to set a budget then do envelope budgeting.

Should You Utilize Envelope Budgeting within Today's Digital Era?

Most individuals find that establishing a budget then putting money aside in separate envelopes for various expenses includes an excellent method of controlling spending. This technique of budgeting permits individuals to have the exact money needed for bills, which may keep you from accidental overspending. But, envelope budgeting will have its downside.

Though this system possesses a multitude of benefits, if you utilize envelope budgeting, you need to constantly go to the ATM or bank, according to Money Crashers. It might be challenging if you work within bank business hours; additionally, it's hard to make envelope budgeting operate unless your whole family is on board. Also, utilizing cash for envelope budgeting will increase the odds that you may accidentally lose cash. However, there now are many sites on the Internet, which permit you to modernize the exact same principles used for envelope budgeting, and even enable you to have a safer and more convenient way to budget.\

As you use envelope budgeting, the whole family must be involved in the budgeting limits and plans for the budget to be a success. If you utilize all cash, yet your partner uses debit or credit cards, it may be simple to overspend. Utilizing an online tool may assist everyone in being on the same page, and also, it'll make it less likely that you'll lose cash because cash might be lost or misplaced.

So you can have a successful budget as you change from envelope budgeting to using tools online you still have to begin the same way. Firstly, you ought to decide how much cash you need in order to pay for your monthly expenses then figure out how much discretionary cash you have every month. Think about how much cash you require every month for your mortgage or rent, for food, for transportation, for clothes, etc. You also should set aside money towards your retirement and an emergency fund.

Mint permits you to establish your own budget based upon your spending patterns, allowing you to check how much you regularly are spending on various items and bills. It's like envelope budgeting because you're able to establish your budget based upon what you routinely spend. You also can plan for one-time costs, and the website permits you to check how much you'll save by trimming back in various categories. It's possible to get alerts for odd account charges, in order for you to know if you're missing cash (unlike when keeping cash inside envelopes and all of a sudden, you are missing $50 bucks).

An additional method of sticking to your objectives and make budgeting simpler includes using a website such as Simple. Your bank account online is going to come with multiple Android apps, and Visa card. With the site's Safe-to-Spend plan, you'll know whether you truly can afford to purchase something or not. Forget keeping money in different envelopes; the tool is able to subtract upcoming expenses from your balance, in order for you to know how much you have on-hand to spend. Also, it'll subtract pending transactions and keep track of the goals you set. This way you do not need to literally check if you have any cash left; you'll know how much you're able to spend.

While the majority of people do not utilize actual envelopes to track their long-range savings, trying to track multiple statements through mail may be challenging. Using a site made to track your investments is an additional excellent method of using digital tools to make life simpler. GnuCash includes a website to try; it permits you to keep track of stocks in addition to costs. Personal Capital includes another option. The more of your monetary details you're able to track on the Internet, the simpler it might be for you to remain on track. There are, of course, security risks while using sites on the Internet, yet most websites prioritize the security of users.

If you're able to get the family on board, think about offering your envelope budgeting routine a paperless upgrade. It is an excellent and safe method of meeting your financial goals.

Action Steps:

Be careful about the debt incurred. You must avoid the worst monetary mistakes if you want to save.

Saving cash is not easy, yet if you take some time to place these 5 steps into practice, you'll be off to a great start.

CONCLUSION

Money seems to be at the heart of most people's problems where ever you go and whomever you speak to. We most certainly can't live without it in the modern world we live in. However, being a slave to money is the wrong approach. We need to become masters of money. That is, we need to master the money we have and not squander it. There are times where we need to spend money but, to often, many people spend their money on things that they do not need or that will only have short-term affects. Learning to shift your mental focus to think more wisely about your Money is essential if you are going to be able to provide a future for yourself and you family.

It's scary to feel like we won't have enough money to support our family or even just ourselves. But the best way to get over that fear is to take positive action steps towards a better outcome. You can use the tips, knowledge and strategies in this book to make those first steps, beginning with, facing up to your financial situation and creating a plan.

Flick the switch in your mind that leads you down a path of taking decisions to help your future self. Take the decision to be sensible, to be conservative, and to save for you and your families future on this Earth.

THE END….

Steven E Dunlop

ABOUT THE AUTHOR

Steven Dunlop is an entrepreneur who sees a bright future. He is a professional author dedicated to studying and executing in peak performance strategies, with a specialty in business, health and the world's best success strategies. He also pursues a extensive range of extracurricular activities that lead him to experience life changing adventures and new discoveries.

Steven has become a master at focusing his energy to deliver world class content that is helpful, easy to understand and enjoyable to read. He was born in 1989 and graduated from Bristol University with degrees in Business   and   English.

Steven   has   been   studying   and   implementing   self development strategies for the last 8 years, spending thousands of dollars and tremendous amounts of time and energy in this endeavor. His two favorite role models are Tony   Robbins   and   Arnold   Schwarzenegger.

"It is in your moments of decision that your destiny is shaped."–Tony-Robbins

22

"Strength does not come from winning. Your struggles develop your strengths. When you go through hardships and decide not to surrender, that is strength."-Arnold Schwarzenegger

"The path to success is to take massive, determined action."-Tony-Robbins

Steven is a reader first and foremost, he is also a fitness enthusiast, long time amateur body builder, and a passionate writer. He enjoys writing on subjects that will truly be helpful to thousands of people. Steven has been very successful throughout his life in competitive situations, such as in sales, track and field, rugby, strength training, running businesses, brewing beer, and anything else that he is currently focusing his attention on. Steven has led many teams to victory over the years and during that time has acquired a powerful set of motivational and leadership skills. Steven attributes his success to his ability to focus his time, energy and strategic thinking skills to a particular goal in a relentless manner until it has been accomplished.

Steven makes a strong effort every day to expand his knowledge so that he can bring you world class content each and every time. You can contact Steven at kindleshack@gmail.com

Thanks for reading!

www.ingramcontent.com/pod-product-compliance
Lightning Source LLC
Chambersburg PA
CBHW070302190526
45169CB00004B/1507